Edition Eulenburg
No. 711

J. S. BACH

CONCERTO

for Violin, Strings and Basso continuo
für Violine, Streicher und Basso continuo
A minor / a-Moll / La mineur
BWV 1041

Eulenburg

JOHANN SEBASTIAN BACH

CONCERTO

for Violin, Strings and Basso continuo
für Violine, Streicher und Basso continuo
A minor / a-Moll / La mineur
BWV 1041

Edited by / Herausgegeben von
Kristina and Christian Pfarr
in collaboration with / unter Mitarbeit von
Achim Seip

Ernst Eulenburg Ltd
London · Mainz · New York · Tokyo · Zürich

CONTENTS / INHALT

PREFACE / VORWORT

We have become used to thinking of Johann Sebastian Bach's concerto writing almost exclusively in terms of the six so-called *Brandenburg Concertos*, which occupy a pre-eminent position both in the concert repertoire and in the purview of musicologists. It is only comparatively recently that the violin concertos – apart from the Concerto in A minor (BWV 1041), the surviving works are the Concerto in E major (BWV 1042) and the 'Double Concerto' for two solo violins in D minor (BWV 1043) – have gained wide currency, and the A minor Concerto, which the literature stubbornly persists in labelling a 'severe' work, has always been somewhat overshadowed by its 'radiant' E major counterpart.

In structural terms both concertos conform to the pattern of the solo concerto[1] as this had evolved in the first decade of the eighteenth century under the influence of Vivaldi and Torelli. This concerto pattern, in turn, derived from the concerto grosso form that had found its ideal-type expression in Corelli. The Vivaldi solo concerto, with its sequence of movements fast–slow–fast, centres on the contrasted opposition between ripieno (tutti) and solo sections,

In bezug auf Johann Sebastian Bachs Konzert-Œuvre hat man sich daran gewöhnt, das Augenmerk fast ausschließlich auf die sechs sogenannten *Brandenburgischen Konzerte* zu richten, die im Repertoire der Konzertsäle und auch im Blickfeld wissenschaftlichen Interesses eine herausragende Stellung einnehmen. Erst verhältnismäßig spät rückten die Violinkonzerte – neben dem Konzert in a-Moll (BWV 1041) sind noch das Konzert in E-Dur (BWV 1042) sowie das „Doppelkonzert" für 2 Solo-Violinen in d-Moll (BWV 1043) erhalten – ins Bewußtsein einer breiteren Öffentlichkeit; der sich hartnäckig in der Literatur behauptende „herbe Charakter" des a-Moll-Konzerts läßt dieses im Vergleich zu seinem „strahlenden" Gegenstück in E-Dur bis heute ein wenig im Schatten stehen.

Beide Konzerte entsprechen in ihrer strukturellen Anlage dem Typus des Solokonzerts[1], das in der ersten Dekade des 18. Jahrhunderts im norditalienischen Wirkungskreis von Vivaldi und Torelli aus der überkommenen Concerto-grosso-Form, die bei Corelli ihre idealtypische Ausprägung erfuhr, entwickelt wurde. Das Solokonzert Vivaldis in der Satzfolge Schnell–Langsam–Schnell bezieht seine Wirkung aus der kontrastierenden Gegenüberstel-

---

[1] The paradigmatic distinction into categories such as 'solo concerto' and 'concerto grosso' follows modern musicological practice, not the terminology of the period. In the first half of the eighteenth century these distinctions were often not made at all, or were made on the basis of the instrumental forces used. Nevertheless, there is a case for using the standard terms inasmuch as they provide a ready and clear means of classification, in the same way that the term 'sonata form' is useful in analysing Classical and Romantic symphonies, string quartets, instrumental concertos, etc.

[1] Die modellhafte Trennung von Gattungsbezeichnungen wie „Solokonzert" und „Concerto grosso" folgt heutiger musikwissenschaftlicher Praxis und nicht damaliger Terminologie. In der ersten Hälfte des 18. Jahrhunderts wurden diesbezügliche Unterscheidungen vielfach überhaupt nicht oder aber aufgrund der instrumentalen Besetzung vorgenommen. Trotzdem erscheint die Sprachkonvention im Sinne einer anschaulichen Systematik gerechtfertigt, wie auch der Begriff der „Sonatenform" bei der Analyse von klassisch-romantischen Sinfonien, Streichquartetten, Instrumentalkonzerten usw. verwendet wird.

with the specifically solo-concerto form being used for the most part only in the first movement, more rarely so in the third and scarcely ever in the second.

At the start of the first movement the ripieno group introduces the ritornello, which is made up of a number of motivic elements and, as its name implies, recurs (usually in shortened form) as the movement proceeds and rounds off the movement in a full reprise. This notion of an instrumental refrain goes back to the Italian operatic aria of the seventeenth century. The solo episodes interwoven between the ritornelli commonly, though not invariably, make use of motivic material from the introductory ritornello. In these passages virtuoso writing for one or more soloists plays a predominant part, with the orchestra merely providing harmonic support, apart from occasional tutti interjections which cannot be ranked as ritornelli proper. Modulations, mainly confined to simple functional steps, are also generally confined to the solo episodes. The use of extended periods and of strongly cadential writing based on circumscribed harmonies is the fundamental distinction between the solo concerto and the concerto grosso.

The basis of the second movement is frequently a ternary A B A song form or a successive form such as A B A B. In some concertos for wind instruments (especially trumpet) the solo part is silent in this movement. The finale – the solo-concerto form included – generally has a dance-like character.

The work of Vivaldi's that was of decisive importance in promoting the spread and influence of the new form in Europe was his collection of concertos *L'Estro Armonico* op. III, published in Amsterdam in 1711. It is quite likely, however, that manuscript copies of compositions by Vivaldi were in circulation in German-

lung von Ripieno (Tutti)- und Solo-Abschnitten, wobei die eigentliche Solo-konzert-Form meist nur im ersten, seltener im dritten und fast nie im zweiten Satz angewendet wird.

Die Ripieno-Gruppe stellt zu Satzbeginn das aus mehreren Motivgruppen bestehende Ritornell voran, das – wie der Terminus besagt – im weiteren Verlauf mehrmals, wenn auch meist verkürzt, wiederkehrt und in vollständiger Reprise den Satz beschließt; die Idee eines instrumentalen Refrains leitet sich von der italienischen Opern-Arie des 17. Jahrhunderts her. Die zwischen den Ritornellen eingeflochtenen Solo-Episoden verwenden häufig, aber nicht notwendigerweise motivisches Material des Eingangs-Ritornells. In ihnen rückt die Virtuosität eines oder mehrerer Solisten in den Vordergrund, wobei das Orchester, abgesehen von gelegentlichen Tutti-Einwürfen, die nicht als Ritornelle zu gelten haben, lediglich für die harmonische Stütze sorgt. Auch die sich meist auf einfache Funktionsschritte beschränkenden Modulationen sind im allgemeinen den Solo-Episoden vorbehalten. Das durch harmonische Straffung ermöglichte kadenzbetonende Musizieren in längeren Perioden unterscheidet das Solokonzert grundsätzlich vom Concerto grosso.

Dem zweiten Satz liegt häufig die dreiteilige Liedform A B A oder auch eine Reihenform wie A B A B zugrunde. Bei einigen Konzerten für Blasinstrumente (vor allem Trompete) pausiert hier die Solostimme. Der Finalsatz trägt – auch in der Verbindung mit der Solokonzert-Form – meistens tänzerischen Charakter.

Vivaldis Schlüsselwerk, das die Verbreitung und Wirkung der neuen Form innerhalb Europas entscheidend förderte, war die 1711 in Amsterdam erschienene Konzertsammlung *L'Estro Armonico* op. III. Mit einiger Wahrscheinlichkeit kursierten aber schon vor 1710 handschriftliche Exemplare von Kompositionen Vivaldis im deut-

speaking territories before 1710[2]. Bach's acquaintance with Vivaldi's work and ideas would appear to date from the first half of his Weimar period (1708–1717), when his personal style was gradually beginning to detach itself from the north German tradition. Forkel writes: 'The violin concertos of Vivaldi, then newly published, served him as one such means of instruction [...] He studied the handling of the ideas, the relationship of one idea to another, the sequences of modulation and sundry other matters.'[3] Of thirteen transcriptions for keyboard instruments which Bach made from Italian concerto sources, no fewer than ten involve Vivaldi; and Vivaldi-style features can also be found in a number of independent works for harpsichord and organ. Unfortunately the bulk of the chamber and orchestral music written in Weimar is either lost or apocryphal. These works could presumably tell us more about the nature and scope of Bach's encounter with Italian formal models. From 1717 to 1723 Bach held the post of Hofkapellmeister in Cöthen. Here there were considerable opportunities and resources for writing orchestral music, and the composition of most of the orchestral works that cannot be dated precisely – including the Violin Concerto in A minor – is therefore commonly assigned to these years around 1720. Conclusive pointers to this widely accepted dating, however, are lacking. Nor do the forces for which the Concerto is written, namely solo violin and ripieno group – the latter comprising first and second violins, viola and basso continuo (i.e. violoncello and/or double bass and harpsichord) – provide a basis for deducing the date of composition.

schen Raum[2]. Bachs Bekanntschaft mit Werk und Konzept Vivaldis dürfte in der ersten Hälfte seiner Weimarer Zeit (1708–17) anzusiedeln sein. Damals begann sich, unter allmählicher Loslösung von der norddeutschen Tradition, sein Personalstil auszuprägen. Forkel berichtet hierzu: „Als eine solche Anleitung dienten ihm die damals neu herausgekommenen Violinconcerte von Vivaldi [. . .] Er studirte die Führung der Gedanken, das Verhältniß derselben unter einander, die Abwechslungen der Modulation und mancherley andere Dinge mehr."[3] Von 13 Bearbeitungen für Tasteninstrumente, die Bach nach italienischen Konzertvorlagen erstellte, entfallen allein zehn auf Vivaldi; Stilelemente Vivaldis lassen sich darüber hinaus in verschiedenen selbständigen Cembalo- und Orgelkompositionen nachweisen. Leider ist der Großteil der in Weimar entstandenen Kammermusik- und Orchesterwerke verschollen bzw. apokryph. Sie könnten vermutlich weiteren Aufschluß über Art und Umfang der Auseinandersetzung Bachs mit italienischen Form-Modellen geben. Von 1717–23 bekleidete Bach die Funktion des Hofkapellmeisters in Köthen. Da sich hier in besonderem Maße Anlaß und Voraussetzungen zur Komposition von Orchestermusik boten, setzt man gemeinhin die Entstehung der meisten zeitlich nicht fixierbaren Orchesterwerke, so auch des Violinkonzerts in a-Moll, in den Jahren um 1720 an, obwohl es für diese weithin akzeptierte Datierung keinen beweiskräftigen Anhaltspunkt gibt. Auch die Besetzung des Konzerts mit Solo-Violine und Ripienogruppe – bestehend aus erster und zweiter Violine, Bratsche und

[2] cf. Walter Kolneder, 'Das Frühschaffen Antonio Vivaldis', *Kongressbericht der Internationalen Gesellschaft für Musikwissenschaft*, Utrecht 1952, pp. 254–262, p. 261
[3] Johann Nikolaus Forkel, *Ueber Johann Sebastian Bachs Leben, Kunst und Kunstwerke*, Leipzig 1802, p. 42

[2] vgl. Walter Kolneder, *Das Frühschaffen Antonio Vivaldis*, in: *Kongreßbericht der Internationalen Gesellschaft für Musikwissenschaft*, Utrecht 1952, S. 254–262, S. 261
[3] Johann Nikolaus Forkel, *Ueber Johann Sebastian Bachs Leben, Kunst und Kunstwerke*, Leipzig 1802, S. 42

VI

Even though Bach took his lead from the Vivaldi model of the concerto, it would be wrong to call the work a copy of this prototype. Certainly the opening 24-bar ritornello of the first movement (unheaded) adheres to convention in a formal sense, with its bipartite opening theme, unfolding sequences and closing cadence. But in the remainder of the movement, until the closing reprise, the schematic division between ritornelli and episodes is largely dissolved. The concertante solo violin, in interplay with the ripieno group, exploits motivic material from the ritornello, whose repeated, abbreviated appearances do not interrupt the solo part but strengthen the close thematic interconnections between the solo and tutti passages.

The *Andante* middle movement in C major develops above a passacaglia-like basso ostinato whose rhythmic severity is relieved by solo cantilenas of triplets. The orchestral parts generate extremely rich harmonies with highly economical means – a Bach speciality, and a feature hardly ever found in the slow movements of the Italian composers.

The final movement, headed *Allegro assai*, is a gigue in 9/8 in which the ripieno parts enter one after another in fugato style. The solo violin takes up the dance-like motion of the ritornello, engaging in virtuoso exchanges with the ripieno group that produce an ever more intense dialogue. In this movement too the use of *durchbrochene Arbeit* makes for an intensification of the musical events, with all the instruments contributing on effectively equal terms.

It is also worth mentioning that Bach arranged the A minor Concerto – as he did other violin concertos, not all of which sur-

Continuo (d. h. Violoncello und/oder Kontrabaß und Cembalo) – läßt keine Rückschlüsse auf die Entstehungszeit zu.

Wenngleich sich Bach an Vivaldis Konzertmodell orientierte, wäre es falsch, das Werk als Kopie des Vorbilds zu bezeichnen. Zwar entspricht das 24taktige Anfangsritornell des ersten (nicht überschriebenen) Satzes mit zweiteiligem Kopfthema, fortspinnender Sequenz und abschließender Kadenz formal der Konvention, doch bleibt in der Folge bis zur Schlußreprise die schematische Trennung von Ritornell und Episode weitgehend aufgehoben. Die Solo-Violine verarbeitet im konzertierenden Zusammenspiel mit der Ripieno-Gruppe motivisches Material aus dem Ritornell, das bei wiederholtem, verkürztem Auftreten die Solostimme nicht unterbricht, sondern die enge thematische Verflechtung von Solo und Tutti unterstreicht.

Der *Andante*-Mittelsatz in C-Dur entwickelt sich über einem Passacaglia-artigen Basso ostinato, dessen rhythmische Strenge durch triolisch geführte Solokantilenen aufgelockert wird. Die Orchesterstimmen entfalten mit sparsamsten Mitteln eine überaus reiche Harmonik, eine Bachsche Besonderheit, die in den langsamen Sätzen italienischer Komponisten kaum anzutreffen ist.

Beim *Allegro assai* überschriebenen Schlußsatz, einer Gigue im 9/8-Takt, setzen die Ripienisten nacheinander in Fugato-Technik ein. Die Solo-Violine greift den tänzerischen Gestus des Ritornells auf und gelangt im virtuosen Wechselspiel zu einem immer intensiveren Dialog mit der Ripieno-Gruppe. Auch in diesem Satz führt die Technik der „durchbrochenen Arbeit" zu einer alle Instrumente als gleichberechtigt begreifenden Verdichtung des musikalischen Geschehens.

Ergänzend sei erwähnt, daß Bach das a-Moll-Konzert – ebenso wie andere, zum Teil nicht im Original erhaltene Violinkon-

vive in their original form – as a harpsichord concerto during his Leipzig period. In the transcribed version (BWV 1058) the work is transposed into G minor.

zerte – in Leipzig zum Cembalokonzert umarbeitete. In der Bearbeitung (BWV 1058) ist das Werk nach g-Moll transponiert.

Editorial Notes

Sources

Editorially speaking, the position regarding the sources of Bach's Violin Concerto in A minor is largely straightforward and unambiguous. The Staatsbibliothek Preussischer Kulturbesitz, West Berlin, possesses a set of parts, partly autograph (Mus.ms.Bach St.145) and two copies of the score in an unknown hand (Mus.ms. Bach P252 and P253).

The set of parts, which has been used as the principal basis of the present edition, probably dates from the year 1730. It can be assumed, as a minimum, that the solo violin and viola parts of movements I and II and all the parts of movement III (apart from the basso continuo) are autographic. The continuo part (which is not figured) has recently been attributed to Carl Philipp Emanuel Bach; Johann Ludwig Krebs, and perhaps other pupils of Bach's, were probably also involved in preparing the set of parts.[4]

Editing principles

Deviations from standard modern notational practice (abbreviations, repetitions of accidentals within the bar, omission of warning accidentals, style of note-stems, 'shorthand' devices such as the use of *Da capo* markings to indicate literal reprise) have been silently altered. Dynamic instructions at the start of movements have been added in square brackets if not given

Revisionsbericht

Quellen

Eine weitgehend klare und eindeutige Quellenlage kommt der Edition von Bachs Violinkonzert in a-Moll entgegen. In der Staatsbibliothek Preußischer Kulturbesitz in Berlin-West befinden sich ein teilweise autographer Stimmensatz (Mus.ms.Bach St.145) sowie zwei Partiturabschriften von unbekannter Hand (Mus.ms.Bach P252 und P253).

Der für diese Edition grundsätzlich als maßgebend angesehene Stimmensatz stammt wahrscheinlich aus dem Jahr 1730. Als autograph dürfen mindestens die Solo-Violine und die Viola zu den Sätzen I und II sowie sämtliche Stimmen mit Ausnahme des Basso continuo zu Satz III angenommen werden. Die (nicht bezifferte) Continuo-Stimme wird neuerdings der Handschrift Carl Philipp Emanuel Bachs zugeordnet; darüber hinaus waren vermutlich Johann Ludwig Krebs, eventuell auch weitere Bach-Schüler an der Stimmenabschrift beteiligt[4].

Editionsprinzipien

Abweichungen von der heute üblichen Notationsweise (Abbreviaturen, Wiederholung von Akzidentien im selben Takt, Verzicht auf Warnungsakzidentien, Halsung, „Faulenzer" sowie *Da-capo*-Verweis bei tongetreuer Reprise) wurden stillschweigend modifiziert. Dynamische Vorschriften bei Satzanfängen wurden, sofern nicht im Manuskript vorgegeben, in ecki-

---

[4] cf. Dietrich Kilian, preface to Johann Sebastian Bach, *Neue Ausgabe sämtlicher Werke*, series VII, vol. 3, Kassel 1986, p. VI

[4] vgl. Dietrich Kilian, Vorwort zu Johann Sebastian Bach, *Neue Ausgabe sämtlicher Werke*, Serie VII, Bd. 3, Kassel 1986, S. VI

in the manuscript source. Ties and slurs added on the basis of analogous passages are indicated by broken lines.

Bach's slurring is well known for its ambiguity and inconsistency and poses a major problem. Phrasings of the three-note groups in the autograph of the third movement, for example, permit of two interpretations throughout: ♩♩♩ or ♩♩♩. The parallel (♩ ♪) rhythm in the viola part would appear to point to the second of these alternatives. Nevertheless, the first version has been preferred here, primarily in order to leave performers with at least the option of the quasi-polyrhythmic interpretation. Bach took for granted the players' ability to make their own decisions in such cases.[5]

Kristina and Christian Pfarr
Translation Richard Deveson

gen Klammern ergänzt; nach Analogstellen ergänzte Bindebögen sind gestrichelt.

Ein grundsätzliches Problem stellt die bei Bach bekanntermaßen vieldeutige und uneinheitliche Bogensetzung dar. Beispielsweise läßt das Autograph im dritten Satz für die Phrasierung der Dreiergruppen in den Violinstimmen durchweg zwei Deutungen zu: ♩♩♩ bzw. ♩♩♩. Die Parallelrhythmik der Bratschenstimme (♩ ♪) scheint auf die zweite Version hinzudeuten. Wenn hier trotzdem die erste Version gewählt wurde, dann vor allem deshalb, weil die quasi polyrhythmische Auffassung dem Ausführenden wenigstens als Möglichkeit offenstehen soll; die Fähigkeit zu bewußter Gestaltung setzte Bach beim Spieler voraus[5].

Kristina und Christian Pfarr

---

[5] On the problems of slurring in Bach generally, and in the A minor Violin Concerto in particular, cf. also Georg von Dadelsen, 'Zur Geltung der Legatobögen bei Bach', *Festschrift Arno Forchert*, ed. Gerhard Allroggen and Detlef Altenburg, Kassel 1986, pp. 114–122

[5] Zur Problematik der Bogensetzung bei Bach im allgemeinen und im a-Moll-Violinkonzert im besonderen vgl. auch Georg von Dadelsen, *Zur Geltung der Legatobögen bei Bach*, in: *Festschrift Arno Forchert*, hg. von Gerhard Allroggen und Detlef Altenburg, Kassel 1986, S. 114 – 122

Einzelanmerkungen

Satz I

Takt		
	4	B.c. Präzedenzfall für Notationen analoger rhythmischer Gruppierungen in allen Stimmen; ♫♫♩ entsprechend auch ♫♫♫♫
	33, 35, 39	Vl. Bindebögen über jeweils erste drei Noten im Takt nicht im Manuskript
	89	Vl. I, Vla. redundante *piano*-Vorschrift autograph
	109	Vl. II Bindebogen im Manuskript über vier Noten; hier analog zur Bratschenstimme
	131	Vl. I Bindebogen von 2. zu 4. N. analog zur Solo-Violine ergänzt
	157	Vl. I Bindebögen analog zur Solo-Violine ergänzt

171 Vl. II, Vla. im Autograph ♩ 𝄾 ; hier analog zu übrigen Stimmen

Satz II

27 Vl. Phrasierung analog T. 13; im Autograph Bindebogen über zweiter Triole, dritte und vierte Triole unter undeutlichem gemeinsamem Bogen

28 Vl. II im Manuskript *forte*-Vorschrift auf letztem Achtel; hier analog zu Bratschenstimme auf erstem Achtel T 29.

41 Vl. Phrasierung analog T 13; im Autograph erste drei Triolen jeweils mit Bindebogen

Satz III

59 Vl. II 1. ♪ (Auftakt für Themeneinsatz in T 60) fehlt im Autograph; hier dem musikalischen Sinn entsprechend ergänzt

68 Vl. I *forte*-Vorschrift im Autograph auf 1. ♪ von T 69; hier analog zu Vl. II

72 Vla. *piano*-Vorschrift im Autograph auf ♪; hier analog zu Vl. 1 und II

141 Vl. I, II, Vla., B.c. im Autograph fermatierte punktierte ♪ als Fine des ersten Ritornells; hier analog zur ausgeschriebenen Solo-Violinstimme

Violino concertato, beginning of the first movement, autograph
Anfang des I. Satzes der Violino-concertato-Stimme, Autograph

Violino concertato, second movement, autograph
Violino concertato, Satz II, Autograph

Basso continuo, second movement, assumed
to be in the hand of Carl Philipp Emanuel Bach
Continuo-Stimme zu Satz II, vermutlich
in der Handschrift Carl Philipp Emanuel Bachs

CONCERTO

Johann Sebastian Bach
(1685 – 1750)
BWV 1041

I.

Edited by Kristina and Christian Pfarr
© 1988 Ernst Eulenburg & Co GmbH
and Ernst Eulenburg Ltd

No. 711   EE 6825

2

4

EE 6825

5

6

EE 6825

II. Andante

14

EE 6825

III. Allegro assai

18

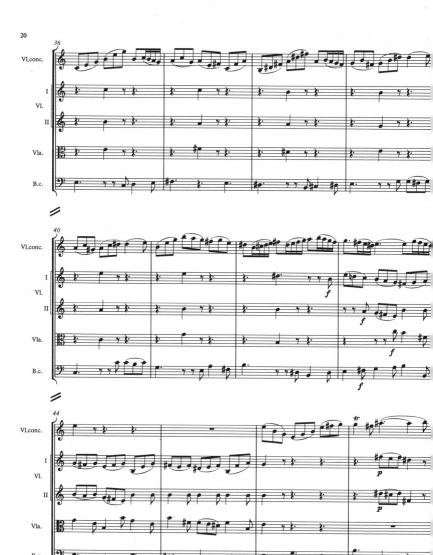

22

EE 6825

24

28

EE 6825

ISMN M-2002-0613-5

9 790200 206135

ISBN 3-7957-6197-2

9 783795 761974

Printed in Germany